SOLANO COLLEGE LIBRARY

D0622937

BOOK SALE
Solano College Library

PR
6052
O38
P4

37749

Bold

A perpetual motion
machine

The Phoenix Living Poets

A PERPETUAL MOTION MACHINE

A PERPETUAL
MOTION MACHINE

by

ALAN BOLD

CHATTO AND WINDUS

THE HOGARTH PRESS

1969

Published by
Chatto & Windus Ltd
with the Hogarth Press Ltd
42 William IV Street
London W.C.2
★
Clarke, Irwin & Co. Ltd
Toronto

SBN 7011 1485 1

© Alan Bold 1969

Printed in Great Britian by
T. H. Brickell and Son Ltd
The Blackmore Press, Gillingham, Dorset

Contents

PS
6052
O38
D4
37749

Dedicatory Poem

FOR MY DAUGHTER, VALENTINA

Thus every day you come alive
Permits the world to spin
And then my mind imposes five
Senses on the specks that drive
The life that you begin.

A growing person in an age
That shrinks from day to night
And I would damn this world, this cage,
If I could not still engage
Some interest in your sight.

The earth turns round and tells that our
Precarious point in space
Is not forever – but these sour
Predictions vanish every hour
We chatter face to face.

June 1967 at Buchenwald

"The stillness of death all around the camp was uncanny and intolerable."
Bruno Apitz, *Naked Among Wolves*

This is the way in. The words
Wrought in iron on the gate:
JEDEM DAS SEINE. Everybody
Gets what he deserves.

The bare drab rubble of the place.
The dull damp stone. The rain.
The emptiness. The human lack.
JEDEM DAS SEINE. JEDEM DAS SEINE.
Everybody gets what he deserves.

It all forms itself
Into one word: Buchenwald.
And those who know and those
Born after that war but living
In its shadow, shiver at the words.
Everybody gets what he deserves.

It is so quiet now. So
Still that it makes an absence.
At the silence of the metal loads
We can almost hear again the voices,
The moaning of the cattle that were men.
Ahead, acres of abandoned gravel.
Everybody gets what he deserves.

Wood, beech wood, song
Of birds. The sky, the usual sky.
A stretch of trees. A sumptuous sheet
Of colours dragging through the raindrops.
Drizzle loosening the small stones
We stand on. Stone buildings. Doors. Dark.
A dead tree leaning in the rain.
Everybody gets what he deserves.

Cold, numb cold. Despair
And no despair. The very worst
Of men against the very best.
A joy in brutality from lack
Of feeling for the other. The greatest
Evil, racialism. A man, the greatest good.
Much more than a biological beast.
An aggregate of atoms. Much more.
Everybody gets what he deserves.

And it could happen again
And they could hang like broken carcasses
And they could scream in terror without light
And they could count the strokes that split their skin
And they could smoulder under cigarettes
And they could suffer and bear every blow
And they could starve and live for death
And they could live for hope alone
And it could happen again.
Everybody gets what he deserves.

We must condemn our arrogant
Assumption that we are immune as well
As apathetic. We let it happen.
History is always more comfortable
Than the implications of the present.
We outrage our own advance as beings
By being merely men. The miracle
Is the miracle of matter. Mind
Knows this but sordid, cruel and ignorant
Tradition makes the world a verbal shell.
Everybody gets what he deserves.

Words are fallible. They cannot do
More than hint at torment. Let us
Do justice to words. No premiss is ever
Absolute; so certain that enormous wreckage
Of flesh follows it syllogistically
In the name of mere consistency. In the end
All means stand condemned. In a cosmic
Context human life is short. The future
Is not made, but waits to be created.
Everybody gets what he deserves.

There is the viciously vicarious in us
All. The pleasure in chance misfortune
That lets us patronise or helps to lose
Our limitations for an instant.
It is that, that struggle for survival
I accuse. Let us not forget
Buchenwald is not a word. Its
Meaning is defined with every day.
Everybody gets what he deserves.

Now it is newsprint and heavy headlines
And looking with a camera's eyes.
Now for many it is only irritating
While for others it is absolutely deadly.
No one is free while some are not free.
While the world is ruled by precedent
It remains a monstrous chance irrelevance.
Everybody gets what he deserves.

We turn away. We always do.
It's what we turn into that matters.
From the invisible barracks of Buchenwald
Where only an unsteady horizon
Remains. The dead cannot complain.
They never do. But we, we live.
Everybody gets what he deserves.

That which once united man
Now drives him apart. We are not helpless
Creatures crashing onwards irresistibly to doom.
There is time for everything and time to choose
For everything. We are that time, that choice.
Everybody gets what he deserves.

This happened near the core
Of a world's culture. This
Occurred among higher things.
This was a philosophical conclusion.
Everybody gets what he deserves.

The bare drab rubble of the place.
The dull damp stone. The rain.
The emptiness. The human lack.

The Point of Love

What does it mean to be born?
Only a few substantial flips around the sun?
Only dependence on one star in infinity?
Only a second in a larger century?
Only a fraction of the ominpotent One?

Or the instigation of a passionate affair.
Or the reason for the beauty of her hair.
Or the centre of her particular universe.
Or the one that makes our death seem less fierce.
Or the deadly enemy of her despair.

But what if she is only human flesh
Destined to decay, to fly only to crash?
Only one in millions, a pointless whim
Of fate, a trick of carbon, an evanescent flame?
A remnant of the sentiment we have to smash?

Or the very point of staying alive
In a place so viciously combative.
Or the stimulation of the brain
Or the one who makes your life your own again
Or the entity that in herself defines love.

The Realm of Touching

Between my lips the taste of nighttime blends
And then dissolves. It is blank as my eyelids close.
For a flickering of time I concentrate on how time ends.

It should be present, the scent of the rose
We bought, though one petal has begun to fall.
Somehow that simplifies the girl I chose.

Night music must be the sweetest sound of all.
It is made to overwhelm with virtuosity.
But every night it is the same pounding on the same wall.

Nocturnal images are said to be the ones that stay
Longest, with exploitation of the dark half-tone.
This I disregard and watch for the day.

A touch in the realm of touching alone
Adds presence to the absence of light.
A clasp of hands, then bodies, my own
And hers, is when I welcome the blindness of night.

A Memory of Death

Nineteen fifty six was a momentous year,
The year of Suez and Hungary and the death
Of my father. I was thirteen. He was forty-nine.
His body stiffened in the quarry for a day or so,
His flesh submerged and became bloated
While I sat at home full of premonitions of his death.
It seemed the most natural thing for him to die,
The fitting conclusion to the warnings
And daily visits from genial policemen.
Four days we waited, then the news. Dead.
Found dead in the quarry. Circumstances unknown.
Cause of death: asphyxia due to drowning.

"William Bold/Clerk of Works/ (Dept. of Agric. for Scot.)/ . . .
1956/ March/ Found drowned in Bigbreck Quarry,/Twatt,
Birsay, about 4.30 p.m. on Sunday 18th/March 1956. Last seen
alive about 6.30 p.m. on/Wednesday 14th March 1956. . . ."

I remember how the letters to my mother brought back
That summer on the farm in Orkney. The cabin.
The cottage. Living between the cabin and the cottage.
It was the one time I had him to myself.
On the farm Hazel used to take me in her bed at night.
I clung to her big body and felt her warm
Limbs. Hazel was kind and rather slow
And she never said much. But each night
She let me share her bed to get the warmth.
She could dribble warm milk down my mouth,
Drive a tractor and decapitate
A hen. Only she could milk the cows expertly,
Gripping their udders with her weather-beaten hands
Laughing as if she had everything anyone could want.

Her presence gave me comfort like a field of corn,
Her voice familiar as the motors threshing,
As the dogs running and barking. Once,
I fell in the cowshed. I stank
With the sloppy excrement plastered all over.
But she threw her big-boned torso round me,
Washed me down and grasped me and smiled
And the sun shone through her mane of hair.
On the same cow she sat me and held me tight.
And at night we would gape at the moon
Silently fixing our thoughts on it, Hazel
With her arms round me, smiling, glowing,
And we would go to bed after porridge and cocoa.

"I can't tell you how sorry I am to hear of your sad loss . . . I pray
that God be with you to give you strength to bear your great loss."

Snick-crack! The shot was fired. Whirr
Of wings and beat of leaves and shadows in the night.
My first time pulling the trigger. The lake.
Undulating blackness catching shreds of light.
I giggled with the sensation of accomplishment.
He winked and grinned. Then into the boat.
Silently we sliced through the black water.
We didn't speak but listened to the ripples.
Then the illegal otter was launched: a length
Of rope decorated with murderous hooks and, sleek
As an otter, the streamlined wood that pulled the rope.
We waited, looking at each other, grinning
Conspiratorially. Then the jerk and pull
And rip! The mouth snaps and the lip pouts
And we've got a trout. A gleaming trout, a trout
Of subtle highlights and I thump its lovely head
Hard against an oar. One down and several
To go. It's up to us. No rush. Our choice.
Guilty – and happy. Cold – but flushed. Two – like one.

At the farm we grilled the trout. They sizzled away
And we slobbered after them. He thumbed to me.
"He'll make a good poacher, this one, some day!"
Cosy and loveable farm, in an hour or so the sun
Will show. The lake will sparkle and we can look
But no one else will know.

"How is Alan? I suppose he will soon be giving work a thought as
well. What a shame to think he doesn't have his Dad to start him
off and such a clever man."

Fiddle music, stomping feet, thrills
Whisky flowing, boozed up to the gills,
Children on the floor and cakes,
Party pieces, old repeated jokes.

Laughter linking kids and wives and daft
Workers clumping joyously on soft
Carpets – kisses innocent as sweets,
Embraces making boys and girls mates.

Secrets shared and little stories told
Peat thrown on the fire against the cold.
An old piano, floorboards worn and dark
And folk united through the heavy work.

It finishes too soon, the morning calls
And blankets cover all internal ills.
A passer-by will see another farm
Oblivious to the life that breaks the storm.

And inside as the shutters shake and creak
A child's eyes eagerly wait for day to break
And look hard for another night like this
Hoping to God the present doesn't pass.

"I never for one minute thought Bill would come to such an end.
I always admired his carefree personality . . . God knows best and
that's all we can say about it."

A lot has been written about Skara Brae,
Vivid first-hand impressions made on the spot.
Full of mystery or a stern sense of history,
Or perhaps some blots scrawled on the back of a postcard
In the pub.
I have a feeling for the place now, rather than a picture.
We had been building a bridge,
Watching the digger devastating the earth,
Waving off the midgies and the clegs.
And after the morning's work: Skara Brae.
I saw burials older than I will ever be.
Remarkable reconstructions of the primitive way of life.
Immaculate patterns of rooms from stone.
The evidence of ingenuity, the suggestion
Of a rigid way of life. And the whole thing
Deep in the ground.
It did not seem amazing or beautiful.
It seemed preposterous in comparison with the farm.
And, perhaps worst of all, it was invaded by new people,
Empty of the old inhabitants. I remember thinking that.
I often think of it now as a silent tomb
For those we never could have known and never try
To know. He was there and it sticks now.
It is redolent with memorial melodies,
A monument made from destruction.
And when I saw Skara Brae
In that clear afternoon, my muscles aching,
I saw it as a member of posterity.

". . . although he was only a lodger his tragic death has upset me
terrible. As you know he was his own worst friend he certainly
was indulging in spirits too much . . . all we can do is bless him
from the bottom of our hearts and remember his happy smile."

I remember his happy smile.
I remember the gaps of missing teeth, the black
Spots on the white, the large lower lip,
I remember the fairisle pullover, green and rust
And white, the ruddy face, the twisted arm broken
In a car crash. I remember the way he walked
Like a big ape
His jacket open, flapping, his eyes bright.

I remember too the alcoholic breath, the false
Euphoria and, after tumbling into chasms of distress,
Depression and confessions of guilt.
These no longer matter, though they seemed to matter then.
They mattered more than they should have. It is so
In Scotland, land of the omnipotent No.

The Sunday-school picnic, the twittering old birds,
The benevolent boy-scouts, the ministers dripping
With goodwill. And the disgrace. He was drunk.
Not objectionable. Just dead drunk.
Sprawled out on the grass focusing on the sky,
With whispers hissing maliciously round about.
They were well pleased with something to feel superior
About, with half a chance to gloat.
"Do you mind Mr. Bold?" What! Grunt!
"Do you mind Mr. Bold not lying there?" Mmmm!
"Do you think you could stand up?"
He tried to, tried so hard, so ostentatiously,
Arms working like a tightrope walker's,
Legs unbuckling – then thump.
Down and out.

". . . it was a huge shock to us all after being here so long with us he was in here so short before having a talk with Jim my husband and the rest of them it was a cold day and I made tea to them all sitting round the fire I think he missed the cabin as they all used to call it he could take a rest when he wanted . . ."

He left the land rover
And stared deep into the water
Thinking life offered nothing more than this liquid pit.
Everything shrunk to the need for action,
For decision. And the audacity of the stars.
Everything at such a distance, people, family,
Friends. And headlong he fell
Slowly into the water
And swore in bubbles
And his eyelids filled with blackness.

The Act of Love

Like an unexpected light in the sky
You suddenly appeared. Only I
Observed you. Only I was able to.
The distance was so great at first.

Then I took you without violation,
With gifts instead, an impulse for creation.
This was fruitful and you grew
In every way. And you burst

And from you slithered a part of you
A part of me and more, yes, so
Much more. Yet only two
Of us quenched the lingering thirst.

For we forgot our bodies in the heat
Of love, merging in an intense sweet
Rage of something beyond the normal few
Words to reach an ecstasy no one had forced.

The Evidence Justifying Poetry

The only difference between the soot that blackens
A sweep's face and the brilliant diamond that sweetens
A woman's flesh is an arbitary pattern of carbon atoms.
When such a substance slackens
It is despised. When it crystallises it sparkles and
Is prized and adored. In that quiet shift of matter
Chimes the whole case for the poet's endless patter.
Equipped only with feelings, he lives to understand.

The Event
for William Redgrave, for his sculptured triptych, "The Event"

I

How did it happen, this event?
Their silent coalescence, captured and exposed.
Their panic, their ephemeral glance,
Their simulation of indifference
Preserved. Clutching and huddling, forced
To face the judgment of a world they represent.

How did it happen, this event?
This timeless spatial portrait of an age.
The eyes screwed up with doubts
The accusing shouts
Directed at the latest useful grudge.
And that woman's fear: is that meant?

How did it happen, this event?
Are these creatures kin or separate?
Do we read them as lies
Do we sympathise
Do we know what we see and ooze hate?
Or do we see this as some alien element?

II

You would never get *people* to pose
Like this. Not for a fortune.
They want the flattering patina
Of schematic beauty, they want
To click neatly, like clips, into
A pre-existing smirk. They want to be loved.

They want the wide clear eyes, the neck
Curving gracefully like a swan's, the hair
Either perfect or slightly out of place
After the best fashion: there must
Be a precedent. But instead
To get three old men bawling out
Their sordid future, to get liquid only
From a bottle of booze, or light
Only from a cigar . . . Nobody is *really*
Like that. Or so they say. But look:
There is a child.
A child, the prime creation, pointing.
Dare we follow to where we want
To go? Only the child points
To a new context, to something beyond
That clinging ambiance of bronze.
Only a child? And we murder children,
Teaching them to learn the limitations
Of a world of man-made limitations.
    It all looks solid, but that only means
Electromagnetic forces have atoms in their grip
So tightly that they oscillate
About fixed propositions.
And the left side of our brain
Commands our right appendages
To shape out, from the imagination
Of the physical, a purely mental
Pattern, so the atoms become flesh,
Flesh becomes breasts, lips,
Fingers, finely finished form.
We see nothing but what we want
To see: intimations of the viscera
Appal us. Yet only in creation
Can we atone for the great crime of complicity
In the familiar daily death
By intention.

Perhaps the only meaningful event
Is suicide. Thousands think so.
To contemplate our planet's future
When the sun swallows us somehow
Empties it of all significance. But a child
Points and a child is the living gamble
In a future. And for that child
Our creation of the future exists
Not in our own likeness, but in a greater one.
This is the reason and the consequence of the event,
The gathering together of our physical resources.
Yes, there are ugly faces, bashed features, murderers,
There is endless violence, greed, terror, death.
But this is the material from which we have
To sculpt what comes next. And there is love
To mount it on. And a child points.

III

Only for a while do we think
Reflect – then walk away
And shut out from our consciousness
The only thing that matters in this day.

This is an event too, this power
Of men and women bravely to dismiss
The vital things as artefacts
And never see the corpse they kiss.

Thomas Galloway
(for A. S. Crehan)

1

A bloody birth in Edinburgh
Among the rented rooms, where love
Intruded, adumbrates new sorrow
For two parents. Not enough
To have to work all day for five:
One drop of love means six to keep alive.
The smoke escapes from stolen coal
And lets long held back tears extol
The sunken cheeks. The room is dark
With light bulbs so expensive
To replace. The struggle will be tense if
Someone doesn't get a job. A lark
Flaps past the window and a little mirth
Comes with it – as if to welcome the birth.

2

Day breaks on the tiny body
That sucks its mother's breasts. Rough
Blankets crowd it from the shoddy
State of room it lies in. Of
All the people in the sullen street
It stands the only chance of looking "sweet",
Yet nothing in its bleary eyes
Suggests it worries when it cries.
It could be lying in a wealthy trance
Or sucking off a duchess. But poor men's thoughts
Do not materialise. Things dominate – cots,
Prams, toys – the unattainables of children's ambiance.
The father turns and scratches his head:
"The way you're bawlin', you'd be better off dead."

3

But baby didn't die despite
The life, the smells, the bread,
The damp, the dark. It survived the might
Of poverty and filled its head
With stuff from books at an early age:
Reading, learning, marking every page.
At school the teachers preached the word
Of God, but even then it seemed a third
Of what they said was insincere;
The rest was poetry badly spoken.
None of the evidence seemed very clear
And all commandments had been broken
In the past. What was called God
Was quiet obedience – for Tam, a fraud.

4

The clouds swept high above day
After day with subtly changing forms.
Below in slums the people may
Be replaced by newer ones. No storms
It seemed could break the upper strata Tam
Galloway kicked against – an Olympian calm
That settled everywhere and everyone.
(As necessary, they said, as heat from the sun).
But through his rags and vulgar speech
Tam measured his mind against the posh
Ones near the street: Siegfried Bosch
May have had the chances – each
To what he can – but if they really pushed
A brain behind that brow, Tam's hopes were crushed.

5

At twelve years Tam succumbed
Into acceptance of his promised fate.
For some time his father had thumbed
Through the local ads in a state
Of slow impatience. Tam would learn a trade
And find out how a home was found and made
A pigsty. "If I could labour all my life
Why should he get more?" Quietly the wife
Smiled to her son. The father's ugly sneer
Stopped her from speaking out the truth;
Better to weep than feel his hand across her mouth.
Better to let him smugly know her fear
Than let Tam suffer. At this the boy
Swallowed happiness, rejected joy.

6

Since the decision was taken
Tam felt his studies were a farce.
His faith in knowledge, badly shaken,
Dissolved into love of clothes; fast cars
Meant more to him than books or learning
And he longed to leave school to begin earning
Money. These years he dribbled in the scum
Of sub-cultural life till he liked the slum
Environment – safe, settled and completely closed.
The open razor replaced Occam in his hand.
Sundays meant lounging on the hot sand
In summer. On weekdays the gang blazed
A trail of petty terror round the neighbourhood:
"Let them lose steam – it's all for the good."

7

They said, but their surprise
When Tam and all his friends appeared
In court was something. It was as if they feared
A scandal – as if all the usual lies
They told of morals and of honesty
Were now reversed. At last they
Shunned the boys, the Jurors, and believed
Their viciousness anarchic. Tam had heaved
Into a warehouse with his friends
And stolen cigarettes. Fear, feet and noise
Combined to raise the Jurors and the boys
Were "apprehended". But courage tends
To mark its man somehow and if the foe
Were as easy to fight as the cops then no

8

Enemy would stop Tam. Say
He thought from time to time, the effort
Wasn't mental action, for it hurt
To think of what he might have been one day
And worse – what still could happen if he tried:
A chance to change the world before he died.
The congeries of circumstances, place
And friends dealt him the joker, not the ace.
If you have started from the very top
It would be easy looking down to want
To work your way up from there. But you taunt
Your fate. It was not easy for Tam to stop
The idea that the cards were down. Understand
The feeling that you're trapped in history's hand.

9

At this time stories raged
About a war in Egypt. Tam's big brother
Was sent out to implement the staged
Morality of shareholders. And the other
Side? An "arab with his finger on our throat",
Or "people making bloody sure they got
The profits from their toil". Tam heard both sides
(His cousin was a Red), but saw the Ides
Of April in events in the world. Beware
Tam, lest your imagined Brutus knife
You. Your mind has fed on life
Before and on the past. You mustn't scare
The crows of introspective terror;
Fear of simulated fear's an error.

10

Feeding now on American trash
In comics, Tam's mind regressed.
He escaped from crime in bursts with Flash
Gordon and the like. He was impressed
By gangsters in the films. Yet at school
Teachers agreed that, really, he was no fool.
He resisted learning – let it pass him by
While none of his would-be mentors asked him why.
The last three years at school were hell
For Tam. Instead of learning Euclid
Or scanning Byron, he would rid
His mind of problems. When the period bell
Rang, school problems had dissolved
But there were more intense one to be solved.

11

Once, staying late at the beach
On Sunday, Tam saw the sun set
On naked beauty and the moon bleach
Her in its pallid light and the wet
Skin glisten. Tam had slept
With Jean but now he felt inept,
Superfluous, and he knew his hold
Would loosen on her. Her cold
Disdain would freeze and loyalty
Would seem absurd. She could hardly feel
Affection for a failure, and no seal
Of childish honour could change that. Royalty
Attracts little girls and since
Jean's schema of success fitted a prince

12

Of learning as well as by name
Tam wasn't in the running.
It struck him that though students had the same
Credentials, intellectually, as he, their cunning
And a kind of smoothness in their talk
And dress cut them off from him. A walk
Home confirmed all that Tam surmised.
Jean thought he would be surprised
When she announced they'd "seen enough
Of one another". Even her very phrase
Suggested she was moon and star struck; the case
Was clear. Tam was nice but *rough*;
Jean felt the need of "better company". Some
Thing told Tam she'd been prompted by her Mum.

13

The point of Jean it seemed to Tam
Was her dislike of anything
Suggestive of her own home,
Her working class environment. Sing
Of houses on the hill and Jean
Will love it. But if she thinks you mean
Dead decrepit houses where an old man peeps
At his life – the sun-drenched slag heaps,
The shafts for humans, the pits, old
Disused railway tracks where rubble
Lies regally – you have asked for trouble.
Jean likes to see them rolled
Back to make room for the essence of her life,
Its latent wealth. To be Tam's wife

14

Would bring her constantly in touch
With the grimy side of her upbringing.
She wanted out of it, and not much
Savvy was needed to envisage Tam bringing
Home the bread – and nothing else.
Jean was ambitious, jealous
Of the wealthy few her sex appeal
Could add her to perhaps. To feel
Tam's big body every night in bed
Was not unpleasant but it meant
Nothing more than pleasure. When Tam spent
His energy on her that was all he had.
She liked his entry well, now he was out:
Her finality left nothing for him to doubt.

15

Tam's body almost ached at first
For Jean. He had not realised
She meant so much. A kind of thirst
For any woman took over, disguised
As pure affection. It was nothing more
Than lust interrupted. He felt sore
Physically in his nether parts after dark
Approached. No one to take to the park.
Her blonde hair became "golden",
Her body "divine" in retrospect. Platitudes
Perhaps, but recent lack of words made moods
Hard to define for Tam. To hold them
Became so difficult that now a book
Held hellish memories, so that to look

16

At a collected Shakespeare or Scott
Annoyed him. He tried to rationalise
This fear of knowledge and fought
The notion that books could prise
Open the nature of a working man.
Life taught much more he argued when
A scholar snubbed him. "Whoat the hell
D'you ken that I dinnae? Well? Tell
Me! You're stuck because you cannae say. . . .
But I can. I've read as well. Thae
Books are for bairns who cannae think
For themselves. I don't want to know
What Shakespeare said. And, oh
I ken your patter a' right . . . ye stink!"

17

Naturally, Tam's case was not made
Watertight. His premises were wrong
And, were they right, his "raid
On the inarticulate" was not strong
Enough to intimidate a first year
Undergraduate. We could not, we fear,
Allow Tam's statements to attain
To scientific status. Yes, he has the brain
But not the intellectual brawn.
Why question if his statements are
Falsifiable in principle. Where
Would that get us just now. Rather than moan
About his present plight you must accept
Tam's state of mind. He is not swept

18

Along on the waves of the class war
Or on the wings of history or on
The winds of change. Far
From framing his thoughts thus, Tom
(As he now likes to be called) is obsessed
With material conditions which *he* cannot test
Empirically. They just loom large
And dominate all he does. To charge
Him with incompetence at this
Stage would be absurd. How can
A working person avoid his tools, how can
He consider problems in an academic miss-
Or-sometimes-hit fashion? Toss
Off school – the teacher is a model for the boss.

Tom's dad was right in one way – getting work
Without qualifications was no walkover.
Tom, a schematic chip of the old block,
Would have to fend for himself. To her
(Jean) he was useless and that sentiment
Was shared by employment
Agencies. To get a trade Tom needed
His leaving certificate. He had not heeded
Those pundits in the teaching staff who told
Him what to expect if he was foolish
Enough to leave without that scrap of paper. Mulish
To the nth degree, Tom thought he was old
In the ways of the world – this at fifteen.
Now, interview after interview, the "mean

Old bastards" who saw him in
His Sunday best to get a "post" smiled
Benevolently. "Mr. Galloway, ten
Young lads have applied for this job. Mild
Weather isn't it. What was I saying?
Yes. You see, the others who applied
Had their leaving certificate. You have tried
Without one. I do not for a moment doubt
Your potential, but, you realise, without
Credentials. . . . It would be unfair
To the others. An exception, I fear,
In this case is out of order. I thought
Everyone left school with something. Why
Not you? You neglected your work. I see. Goodbye."

After weeks of the same routine
Tom felt the weight of those outside
And his own impotence. If he should sign
For any job it seemed that all his pride
Would vanish. At school his abstract potential
Was held in awe. It was not essential
Then to meet people in the street and
Tell them, "I'm no longer at school". "Grand",
They always said, "and what do you intend
To do? Have you started anything
Yet?" Tam answered: "Well I can't quite bring
Myself to a decision. I'll have to mend
My ways, you know." He could mimic so well
The posh voice. "I'm thinking though – like *hell!*"

22

On his own in the country just beyond
The city, Tom would watch the silver birch
In Autumn and, reflected in the pond,
The sycamore, the rowan tree, the larch
Lurching in the wind; and then the leaves,
Red, rust and brown, would rustle on his sleeves.
The green patches would be covered
Soon by dead leaves. Those who suffered
In the world Tom compared to Autumn
Leaves, and when he saw the grass recede
He fumbled for the thought of greed
And cruelty winning. And so from
The victory of the dead, the thing
Was clear. In life there was no automatic Spring.

The Drunken Boat

(From the French of Arthur Rimbaud)

As I passed down impassive rivers
I lost my haulers from the narrow coasts:
Screeching redskins made targets of their shivers
And nailed them naked to their coloured posts.

I was indifferent to the men on board
With English cotton or with Flemish grain.
When they were done for – like the previous horde –
The rivers did the bidding of my brain.

Splashing furiously in the thunderous tide
I, last winter, mindless as young boys,
Got free! Unmoored peninsulas have cried
For mercy from my strident triumphant noise.

The tempest blessed me waking on the sea
And, lighter than a cork, I danced on waves
Cursed as breakers of victims, constantly –
Ten nights without a stupid beacon's blaze.

Sweeter than sour apples' flesh to fine
Kids, green water flushed through my pinewood hull
And took the stains of vomit and blue wine
Along – scattering rudder and grapple.

And from that time I floated in the Poem
Of the Sea, full of stars and milky white,
And guzzling green azures; where ghastly foam
Ripples, a drowned dreamer sinks out of sight;

Where blotting out the blueness – mental fires
And panting rhythms, the day's glow above,
Stronger, more vast than alcohol or lyres –
Ferment the bitter red fluids of love.

I know skies thrashed with lightning, maelstroms, troughs,
Surfs, currents; I know the evenings
And dawn arising like a flock of doves
And know the substance of imaginings.

Seen low suns bespattered by mystic spray
Lighting up a solid mass of violet,
At times like actors in an ancient play;
Waves moving like shutters shuddering shut.

I have dreamed of the green night of dazzling snows,
The kiss climbing slowly to the sea's eyes.
The circulation of unheard-of-force;
Risen to yellow-blue songs of Phosphorus.

I've tagged for months as the swell crashed
Into the reefs, like herds of crazy cows;
Astonished that these shining feet have smashed
To silence the great ocean's gaping mouth.

Know I've struck incredible Floridas
Where flowers mingle with panther's eyes in
Human skin. Reins of rainbows can pass
To sea-green crowds under the horizon.

Enormous marshes rise like traps – invite
Leviathans to perish in the reeds.
Great sheets of water in the midst of quiet
And distances dissolving in the deeps.

Glaciers, suns of silver, waves of pearl,
Burning skies! Hideous hulks buried
Where massive vermin-ridden creatures swirl
In murky odours and a tangled weed.

To children I'd have loved to show the swift
Dolphin, or fish of gold that seem to sing.
Foam of flowers flattering my drift
Or insubstantial winds lending a wing.

Occasionally, sick to death of zones and poles,
The sea, whose sobbing gave my boat some peace,
Showed shadowy yellow sucking flowers until
I wearied like a woman on her knees.

I was an island, my beach buzzed to sounds
And droppings of battling birds with clear eyes.
I can sail, when across my severed bonds
Drowned men blunder into sleep, capsize!

I, a lost boat, in the hair of inlets,
Tossed by the hurricane to the stratosphere;
Irrelevant to Monitor or Hanse ships,
A wreck, a drunken carcass, full of water;

Free, steaming, rising from purple mists,
I who drilled the rosy wall of sky
Which has a jam exquisite to good poets,
Snotblue lichens mixed with sunlight; I

Who ran, crackling with electricity,
Mad stick, escorted by black sea-horses,
When Julys were cudgelling with cruelty
To make violent funnels from deep blue skies;

I who trembled, when from fifty leagues
Behemoth roared, and maelstroms fed on sweats;
Eternal spinner of static blueness,
I ache for Europe's ancient parapets!

I've seen archipelagos of lights,
Islands whose insane skies draw the sailor;
Do you exile yourself in endless nights,
You million golden birds, the future's power?

And now, I have wept too much! The dawns break
My heart. Moons are odious, suns austere:
Sharp love has passed over and left me weak.
O let my keel crack! Let me disappear.

If Europe has water I want, it is
A cold black pool at twilight where softly
A child sits full of sadness and launches
A boat, frail as a butterfly in May.

No more, bathed in your inertia, waves, can
I sail behind the cotton carriers' bulks.
Nor tolerate the arrogance stitched in
Flags; nor bear the ugly gaze of hulks.

"Our everyday experience even down to the smallest details seems to be so closely integrated to the grand scale features of the Universe that it is wellnigh impossible to contemplate the two being seperated."

Fred Hoyle, *Frontiers of Astronomy*

"Can I be sure that, in leaving all established opinions, I am following truth? and by what criterion shall I distinguish her, even if fortune should at last guide me on her footsteps?"

David Hume, *A Treatise of Human Nature*

"There is a place
(If ancient and prophetic fame in Heav'n
Err not) another world, the happy seat
Of som new Race call'd *Man*"

Milton, *Paradise Lost II*

"This, it seems to me, is the test: whether a man can bring himself to lie beside a leper and warm him with the glow of a lover's heart."

Rainer Maria Rilke, *The Notebooks of Malte Laurids Brigge*

"For I will conclude by repeating the confession that in spite of the ingenious reasonings of many contemporaries, I am still much inclined to believe that I have ideas, and that without them I and other men would know even less than we do – would, to be precise, know nothing at all."

Arthur O. Lovejoy, *The Thirteen Pragmatisms*

The Tomb of David Hume
A Speculative Poem

Your name is first
In the names of celebrities
Interred in the Old Calton Burying Ground,
And I'm afraid even David Allan
Couldn't really come near you.
But we'll let him rest
Or what is left of him:
The Continence of Scipio
The Origin of Painting
The Connoisseurs
The Murder of Rizzio
All more vivid than the putrefying
Goo beneath the earth
Beneath the sky.
We'll leave the so-called
Scottish Hogarth
A gallery piece in
Edinburgh and Glasgow
And turn to you
As you keep turning
In your grave
Your Roman Tomb
Leaving it to posterity
To add the rest.
You were born
Six days after me
232 years before
And, man, how you've grown!
You live for thousands
And, through their work, millions
Who've never heard of me
And never will.

You have made and make
A mighty sense
In a world of monstrous consequence.

But what of you is there
In this death-stilled air?
What matters does not hide
Beneath this hillside.
Your human essence won't be found
Underground.
We must shake off the dust
The gravel
And move far
From those who rest
Contented in their Sunday best
And nod
And plod
And fume
At David Hume
Whom no religion
Can be based upon.

Let us say it together, man
Is the measure of all things, Man
Is the measure of all things. Not
Abstract models tested psuedo-scientifically
By the shedding of the common blood
Or systems where the end
Never comes but the end
Justifies humane slaughter, reluctant fratricide,
Present misery enjoyed
For future happiness.
Nothing should impel a man to sacrifice
His only possession – his life – for wise
Words well whispered after the event.

Nothing can hide the dead
Not even the living.
If future generations thank him for his blood
What good
Does that do
You?

But stay upright
It is not my intention
To kick your feet under you
To tread
Indiscriminately on your meaning
Or put your soles
Where your eyes should be.
You can do without.

There was Hegel standing on his head
You disturbing Kant's dogmatic doze.
Marx and Engels painting the town red
And Popper holding Cleopatra's nose.

Is it the colour you mind?
I am not painting everything black
In the modern world. I'm not a blind
Dog sniffing. I can see. No academic hack
Me who makes his money obfuscating work
Made clear by you. You destroyed dark
Forces, impeccable syllogistic proofs
Of how the world and all that's in it moves
Discreetly at the bidding of a God.
How odd
That seems now I can testify
That you would be surprised
To know that miracle-maniac Christ
Means less today than then. Would
You have wanted it so?

No one really
Believes in the mealy-mouthed
Pretensions of the church.
The search
You led for an account of man
Has still just begun.

You have found me out.
One minute I praise
You then I denigrate. Doubt
This age when no one says

Privately how sick we all are
And proud of it and show it
Publicly. I can hear
No one but a poet

Emerge to shoot
Holes in our brain-cans
Of liquid rubbish. Thought
Must begin again to sense

Some truth. Money
Is the root, branch and bloom
Of our evil. So say
All of us. Your tomb

Resounds. I name
Everything while saying it,
I claim
You while you hate

My poem to put you right
About my time in the language
Of my time, in the bright
Shadows of my age.

I said a poet. I didn't say a bird.
I emphasise that I repudiate
All the stuff the nancy-boys create
By accident. I won't include a word

About my soul, my underwear, my third
Experience, or bore you with the great
Significance of what I dream. My late
Ancestors mean little – and so I guard

You for the most important thing of all:
What man is making of his life and that
Of others whom his actions determine.

I won't allow a few to live like vermin
While the mob takes everything thrown at
Their heads. Come on! We'll make them rise, not fall!

The grass withers at my feet
And the big bulb of an orange sun
Eight minutes old
Mellows me in amber.

You are the genuine article Hume
Alive with truth
Which is here no abstraction
Merely a convenient noun
Which later we'll explore.
Nothing about what you mean to me
Nothing sad or young is convenient
For me. I will not pour emptiness on your shrine.

Yours is no marmoreal monument.

Let us take it that you know
What I don't believe in.
I don't believe in the priority
Of money caked with the flaking blood
Of innocents. I don't believe
In thousands investing in the deaths
Of millions. I don't believe
In the dirty work done by this country
And by others or those who bid
The dirty work done to others
As they would not have it done
To themselves. I don't believe
That we believe our presence
Far from home is divine.
Or in the burns inflicted
On the fingers or the quaking
Joints of the terror-stricken flesh
Proclaiming sensitivity
Or the boot in the spine
The fist in the belly
The club butt in the balls
The heat the cold the damp the drab
The black lonely pitiless pit.
It's got to be done, they tell us.
When are we going to reply?
And prove that humans still exist
And can resist
The military exigency
Carefully planned.
What is done in the name
Of liberty:
Liberty
All things
To all men.

I have the same goal as you
A Differentiated Society
By which I mean
A collection of people
Working for themselves
Through others
And through themselves
For others.
Not a compromise
A mere *modus vivendi*
But an affirmation of diversity
On the condition that the spice
Is stronger than sentimentality
And twice as tender.
He who sneers from the social sidelines
At the impulse of non-politicians
Will inherit our rage.

There is the man
So like a ghost
That if there were any
He would be that which
They deviated from,
The proto-norm.
Beware the disembrained body
The content-less form
It can exist:
The knee the elbow and the fist.
Especially the last.

We have to face up to certain peccadilloes,
Nugatory issues often swept aside,
For in the framing of hypotheses
We guess and try to falsify the guess,

Record sense-data after the creative event,
And conjectural cowardice exists
As well as consequential diffidence.
The sun is not immortal
Though suns in general may be
And so we must die the death
As an earthbound species.
Now we matter more than asteroids
Whirling round supporting nothing
But death
Or distant suns collapsing
Centuries ago.
So posterity will hate the coming
End and copy us, as we grotesquely parody
A more hierarchic past, instead
Of acting out the present. The past
Has happened, we create the present
But the future is ahead.
Chemistry is so important.
The conversion of hydrogen into helium
Sounds easy, even common, so easy
It sounds as if we were ill
At ease with science, as if we dangled
Figures for your fun. Do not be fooled.
Life will become rare and then extinct
Because the sun is heating up.
Two or three thousand million years from now
No one will remember us because
There won't be anyone to do
The remembering.
Our sun is too big for us to cope with
And it is going to grow
While we glow and bubble in the oceans
And melt through no fault of our own.

Such a young small star, our sun;
So kind but in the end
Indiscriminately destructive.
In the beginning was hydrogen
And it will outlive men.

How much we make of our metaphysical fiddling
Instead of seeing life as something following
A shower of stars condensing out of clouds of gas
And planets moving, and great suns turning in galaxies.
We anthropomorphise immediate nature
And trivialise the wonder of the earth
By pretending that it dropped ready made
From the fidgeting of a self-made God.
A God! A backward dog! A word this age
Inters itself in. So much supersitition
Which reduces the miracle of life;
Not enough dissemination of the real.
The important task you set
Of making a meaning out of life
By making it accessible to all
Has been retarded. The Enlightenment
Believed all was possible, all meant
To fall into places like a perfect jigsaw.
The dark Romantic era passionately held
The ultimate unknowability of the world.
Well we know the arrogance
In this belief of humility.
We know we may know everything to know
And what we'll never know we'll never know.
So many people exercise their brains
At the expense of themselves, growing pains
Merely.
How marvellous to see a world beneath a leaf
Or discern a conflict underneath your feet
Among the insect world. This worm

That writhes in pain through the dust
Feels nothing when we patronise.
If anywhere, the message in the skies
Is the real message. How telling
To interpret ourselves as larger
Brighter animals and smile
Indulgently as if the whole thing were a joke.
It is no joke. An avenue of lime trees
Conceals an ant-like universe. Why tease
The meaning to mean more than that?
It is the telescope and the microscope
Not the microscope alone that shall colour
Our vision.
Our earth is four and a half thousand million
Years old and still
The recent life upon it is intent
On self-destruction. There are more
Ingenious ways of imitating suns than blasting
Human beings to obscene fragments.
Our sun is still young
And small, newer than the red giants
Who live a fifteen thousand million year,
The age of our galaxy with its twenty
Cosmic curtsies. But wait:
No birthday presents yet.
We are indifferent to the life
Upon our planet, as a species we
Do not cohere but could.
Human. The universal view
Is something that must come, after you
Achieve a world-view and care
For the sufferings of others, not
Passively and smugly. Active and hot.
A supernova does not exist
For a child of the Indian lower-caste

Girl, because the child will not get past
It's second year. The way it twists
Its face in pain tells you
As if you didn't know
That nothing is inside its mind
But food
That should
Be in its blood.

It darkens. How we sadden as our planet
Leaves the sun again for half
A revolution. How we fear
The dark, the turning-away.
We hunger for the glare.
This way we share our world.
Only this way?

To particularise too often means
To parochialise, and interest people
By the uniqueness of what happens around you.
I know it's different in Peking
Where millions move as one and sing
As many, where callisthenic expertise is shared.
They sloganise for peace. Or in Red Square
Or in New York. The differences are there.
Who could find Bernini in the dank squares
Of Georgian Edinburgh, or spot the Coliseum in the air
Around our bits of classical pastiche?
From London to Paris, Bond Street to Wall Street,
Fashions may change in painting or in clothes,
But forget the twenty-one inch version of the truth,
Forget the hegemony of televisual views
And study for yourself. It's not what's strange
And alien about people, but what they share

That interests me. In Amsterdam
I saw a sun set on the quiet canals
And the lights ripple on the colder water
And the going in of many harlots.
I also saw the poor people and the faces
Making clear that hell was here – and that was there.
I have seen and heard things that seperate
Man from man, but nowhere does it justify hate.

And everything I do depends on the
Co-operation of infinity.

Have I defaced your tomb?

The grass cannot erase the human mind.
Nature cultivates what men command.
It honours always the attempts to find.

The sun drenches the twigs and branches twined
About your grave. It does not understand.
The grass cannot erase the human mind.

A systematic lucid work you signed
Still-born, but it grew mighty and grand.
It honours always the attempt to find.

Your florid features made your colleagues blind
To what was truly noble. Through your hand
The grass cannot erase the human mind.

It matters little now that you were kind
And others less so who crumble like sand.
It honours always the attempt to find.

You are fresh while academics grind
Thought to a halt and slobber – slow and bland.
The grass cannot erase the human mind.
It honours always the attempt to find.

In a city of shocking contrasts
You are honoured.
Our once Hume-hating university
That turned you down alive
Now makes amends
And the new men in the new building
Pretend they have solutions.
It is not true.
A Hume tower to learning sounds ideal
But our empirical distrust of the ideal
Is sound in this instance.
Learning how to crawl and polish
Spit and shine
How to live with decoration
Is hardly apposite.
In the damp lurid atmosphere
Of the misnamed homes
So many of our people live in
There is no mention of Hume.
There is no mention of anything
Speculative.
There is only the hanging mouth
The bloodshot eyes, the repetition
Of a few blunt words
And blunter acts.
And this is made by men
Who make so much,
And we can make them want
To change.
This is all a writer can do:
Inspire and then expire.

But when the workmen stood up to the clouds
And built the structure called after you
And earned the admiration of the crowds
And earned their contact with a golden blue
Sky, then their limit. As they hung in the air
Did they ask what was an honest share?

The place has changed.
The craggy outlines of the castle
Still cut into the sky
And the first planned city
Is unique in parts.
But given life without the means to live
Is unacceptable. The means are there,
There is simply something stopping happiness
And it can be moved and removed
Cut out
Changed.
The monetary mentality, the accumulative passion,
Have to be used for other things
Than ruining men.
Accepting that men are not equal
That brains are not shared evenly at birth
We must nevertheless ensure
A chance for all and never take
Our chance at the expense of others.
This is what it's all about:
Freedom as it means that for every
Man.
No point asking a man in a cage
To exercise his free will
To act
To implement his essence
To put existence first.

That comes after
Physical release.
Remember that, please.

There is one aspect of empiricism I hate
Although I'm not blaming you for it.
It tests by one experience alone
And smugly sweeps aside the possibility
Of crippling limitations. To verify a statement
Like "Asia exists" is simple: look and see,
Or record evidence by known observers.
But let no one assume
That what's before our nose is vital
Just because we can smell it.
I can say that war is wrong and you agree.
But some men, in the name of common sense,
Put it down to human nature. As if that
Were something fixed for good – or bad!
As if human nature sprang intact and grew
Steadily without changing, without reference
To social change and historical events.
Human nature is made, created
By houses, jobs, conditions,
Families, traditions,
Assumptions in the first place
Of what nature is.
Your projected science of common sense
Your science of man proceeds by tests
By testing by experience.
Yet in your name or in the name of sense
Fools assert a right to indifference.
You knew there was one kind of thought
Epistemologically sound – the human kind.
You grasped "the supine indolence of the mind"
And scorned "its rash arrogance,

53

Its lofty pretensions, and its superstitious
Credulity."
And knew that those who claimed to know
What is good for us are frauds
Little self-styled Gods
Relying on our gullibility
Our servility
And acceptance of all things that sound
Profound.

There are things it wastes our time to talk
About, but we must talk about the way
The people talk about them. There is no God
And no surprise at that. No set date
Can be arranged for the creation,
For the clean conception of the universe.
The surprise is that so many
Want to hold the hand of God
Want a blankness to embrace them.
Social organisation so far takes
No account of the need for people to help
People. This blank, this God, can be replaced
Not by religious atheism or agnostic spiritualism
But by human aspiration. Replaced
It must be. No bleak blank hole
Should be shoved in its place
No smiling politician's face
Should shine instead of grace.

The British
Do not recognise anguish
Officially.
But now
Sleeping dogs rise and bite
Dogs and men
In the night.

The ostentation
Will serve. The glory of life
Will endure in a majestic coalescence
Of all artistic essence.

From the cell to the cell
From the single cell
Containing all the vital information
Given, not God-given, but given
By extra-human factors, to the cell
Of our own creation, the state
We live in that we bow down to
And mumble deferential praise to
And sacrifice our lives, our loves,
Our confidence in choice for.
Yet this larger cell
Is organised morally,
Philosophically, legally,
To aid the survival of the self-styled fit,
The richest, the most ruthless, or the idiot
Ones who arrogantly inherit the rich earth,
Who make the rules we live and die by,
Rules selective and exclusive
Favourable to a minority participating
In matters of moment.

From the cell to the cell
From the single cell to the multicellular
Multifarious, glorious forms of life
We know, to the single cell
We live in and die in.
Imagine that one life is urgent
And important. Imagine
That intelligence can act for itself.

Imagine that conspiracies are not unknown
And act against ourselves. Imagine
There is no obligation to obey a law
Because it is a law
Made up by lawyers who have property.
Imagine they have no right to punish
You or rule your life. Imagine
Your are free within a matrix
Of coincidence
Free to choose from various alternatives
Free to die alone and unabetted
Or live with others like you.
Imagine you can ask
Questions at every turn and do.
Imagine this and we create
A possible world and one we can create.

While radio waves penetrate deep space
And men count objects in their telescopes,
Red giants, white dwarfs, and the colossal race
Of galaxy from galaxy, men's hopes

Are centred on themselves. They cannot trust
The sky to bring them peace. A luminous
Asteroid scraping near the sun has crust;
Some men have not. To man, the numinous

Object that matters is his own body,
Its health, its chances of survival. Tell
Men they are unimportant in the way

Abstract man is important and the spell
May break. If so, no more satiety
For the law-givers, for the poor, piety.

We must grasp the importance
Of the future, for the future
Does not exist yet. It is not there
Ready made, intact, waiting
For us to sidle up on rusty rails
And carry on the line.
It is not a dimension we move in,
It is the continual motion of all worlds.
And we cannot know the next instant for sure.
Those who invest in equity shares
Do not represent the highest stage
Of human growth. They exist
Because confusion and cowardice
Combine to separate the millions,
The once superdense solidarity
Of mankind. Common goals
Must be scored.
We must destroy the feeling
Growing up of hopelessness, the surrender
To extra-human forces for I say
We don't believe in them.

Is it possible that I see clearer
In the dark? Has the sun
Gone out of sight and left me
Brilliant on my own?
It almost seems like it.

When I was unconcerned with art,
Oblivious to the sharp wrench of the heart
And surge of the brain when caught
And urged to sing to others not
What they see but what they could –
Then it was common, if a little crude,
From some sand-brained boy to note

What chance remark of mine to quote
Back at me gleefully and say:
" 'I like the way the sun warms me today'.
See? Get it? Way: today. A rhyme.
You've made a rhyme." For the umpteenth time
He'd grin and show the gaps between his teeth
And freckles on his mottled brow, the Leith
Superscruff, the passing man, the human happening,
The one too humble to be suffering,
And say: "You are a poet
And you don't know it."

He thought it hugely funny, too
Much to take upright, too true
To underestimate. The body bobs
Along the middle, and the sobs
Of laughter gobble in his throat.
A happy day, an inexplicable instant
Of communication, not significant
Or serious, or subtle, but sad
Because irretrievable. To be glad
And share it is compensation-plus
For the death that lives along with us.
Oh, you sandy-haired devil,
You emblem of my youth, uncivil
Angel of my innocence, my daft
Optimism, believing that the craft
Of life was to avoid all harm
To us. Nothing hurt, no alarm or fears
Of accidents, no tears
Or anguish at the appalling knowledge
That it hurts to be happy, for a wedge
Of cosmic indifference ends our love
For her we love when we then move
To complete and endless ecstasy and share
Every atom of each other and care

For every particle of life in her.
It is the pointless universe, the far
From perfect state of life, that far
From unique existence that lets
The unhappy man thrive. He gets
What he wants, almost. Most
Happiness, for alone he has lost
Nothing and has nothing to lose
But himself which in itself is worse
Than nothing. Only the other
Matters. Only the chosen brother
And lover matter. They make
The man himself. They break
Him when they die. Only they.
They are himself. He needs
Them as the scattered seed
Needs planting and the climate to grow.
He needs them as the flow
Of water needs to rush
Forever to sustain the darting fish,
Or as the brightest star
Depends on us remaining where we are,
Madly looping round the sun.
We know we are not the only one
Life-supporting planet but we act
As if we were. Respect the fact
That we exist in time and cannot wait
Thousands of years for a response
From nowhere in the world. Sense
Decrees we must do it, but keep
It incidental to our own leap
For something heavenly on earth.
Emotional hierarchy is still worth
A wonder. Let us grow
Outwards to the depths of space and throw
All preconceptions to the ground.

But revere life, whatever is found.
However commonplace our species feel
In centuries, remember: we are *real*.

I saw that sand-brained lad again.
But he had aged. His brain
Was sculptured in relief of skin
On that once simple brow. His grin
Was feeble and concealed malicious thoughts
That stilled the twinkle in his eye. Lots
Of questions came and went. His teeth
Were false now like his death
At 24. He was no ghost
But only killed in will. A lost
Person, an inhuman human,
A title, anything but a man.
He had a car, a house, a child, a wife
He hated but put up with. Life
Was so-so he sneered – as if so-so
Meant hell. Could he not go
Away from it? With bills to fear!
A house to furnish! A brat to rear!
I mentioned all the days
Of clear-skied youth. His gaze
Was ugly. "We used to talk
Of poetry and if a crack
Could rhyme, remember what I said?"
I nodded. "A poet
And you don't know it."
I forced a little laugh
But he was past that now. If
I had photographed his hate
It would develop an all-negative plate.
At this I chuckled, then he turned and roared it:
"*I* am a poet, but I can't afford it!"

I am leaving now. It is clear.

The Trifid Nebula to my green eyes
Looks like an aged pundit gazing down
At worlds of mortals. I see a frown
And tilted head and folded hands; a wise
Old meditating gentleman who tries
To do his best but gets weary. A crown
Of stars suspended to his left: a gown
Of white silk wrapped round him. He nods and sighs.

I know I see like this because I use
A heritage of seeing to direct
All shapes into a schematic pattern.
I know that man's great task is to unlearn
These modes of seeing, that he must expect
The unexpected. But what does he lose?

We move in five dimensions you must know:
First, revolving; second, orbiting the sun;
Third, tied to the sun in unearthly slow
Galactic revolution; fourth, the one

That splits astronomers, our rapid flight
From other galaxies; and fifth the way
We walk about on earth – the speed of light
Not being in our picture of the day.

But I believe there is another trace
Of movement that has some significance
To our minute position in all space:

This is a moving dependent on chance.
It is the way a look, a touch, can give
An absolute necessity to live.

Kafka's Grave

I went to lay a stone on Kafka's grave
In Prague. I wanted to make some gesture.
I wanted to leave something, to be sure
Of posthumous connexion, and thus save

Complete eclipse, invading this enclave
Of total brilliance, foreign anywhere.
In Kaprova Street, the Old Town Square,
Jewish Cemetery, family grave.

And so this wise city with its facades
Obscured, with its great things only perceived
Behind successive layers, its charm in part

Its architectural anarchy, its art
Persistent as pulsating stars, invades
And conquers. Force without physique believed.

The End

The word is almost dead. The last smile
Has flickered from the last face.
The sun scatters light over this heap
And the spinning earth crashes into night.
From distances too great ever to be thought
Nothing changes. No one sighs. Nothing breaks,
Though countless suns shine on and age.
We were a people aching for experience
And dying from it too. Now it is accomplished.
Perhaps not yet in fact, but certainly
In principle; and all the meretricious junk
That constitutes our life cannot disguise the end.
It was strange to go through birth to learn
To despise death and then later to concede it.
Can you remember? How the sensory ecstasy
Of growing glorified everything extraneous?
That fish that glistened only for your hook,
Those birds that seemed to fly for you, flowers
Reserving their minor miracles complete in every sense,
Animals panting at your touch, vegetation caressing
You? It was the same for me.
But something happened to change that, to change
Our world into a segment of a fragment,
And happiness became the thing we knew
Could never last. And so the moon, the sun,
No longer mattered but became
Undistinguished lights. Ugly because seen
By no one. What is special apart from life?
And that is gone. Do I anticipate?
Perhaps in time, but time is happening.

This time we're all in it together.
And then I'll tell you, I'll be able to,

How I loved you all, how my faults
Were only faked, how I appreciated every one
Of you. There won't be time unless I say it now
But there's a taste that holds me back
You understand. That's all I have to say.

SOLANO COLLEGE LIBRARY